ﰔ THE SINISTER SH
TRANSLATION OF
FRACASTORO'S *SYPHILIDIꜱ*
SIVE DE MORBO GALLICO
LIBRI TRES BY WILLIAM VAN
WYCK

ﰔ The Primavera Press, Los Angeles. MCMXXXIV

TO

LEON JOSIAH RICHARDSON

WHOSE

GENTLE MANLINESS

AND

PROFOUND SCHOLARSHIP

I

ADMIRE GREATLY

TABLE OF CONTENTS

LIST OF ILLUSTRATIONS

* Courtesy of The National Library, Paris.
† Courtesy of Monsieur Avalon, editor of AESCULAPE, a journal of medical history, published monthly in Paris.

THE SINISTER SHEPHERD

HIERONYMVS   FRACASTORIVS

De Larmessin scul.

JEROSME FRACASTOR.

INTRODUCTION*

AD YOU *lived in the troubled days of the sixteenth century, and happened to be in Verona about the year 1535, in all probability, as it happened to Charles V, your guide might have stopped you in your stroll about the city, to point out to you one of its most illustrious sons.*

Little, thickset, with wide shoulders, slightly pugnosed, with brown eyes, with black hair and long drooping moustaches of the same color, you would have been struck by his looks as he stood before you for a few seconds, biting his upper lip. No one could say that this man did not attract attention.

Such was Girolamo Fracastoro.

The contrast between his cold and distant approach and his charitable devotion, had made him a popular figure in Verona. His talent as a poet, his encyclopaedic knowledge, particularly in medicine, brought him celebrity throughout Europe. Furthermore, his very name was a bit legendary.

At his birth, in 1483, was not his mouth closed so that a surgeon was obliged to separate the lips?

As an infant, had he not remained safely within the arms of his mother when she was killed by lightning?

His father, Paolo Filippo, who loved him to the exclusion of all else, had had him exceptionally well educated, and besides, the lad was so gifted, that when he was barely

---

* This introduction is a translation of an article by Dr. Albert Garrigues, entitled: *Fracastor, Chantre de la syphilis,* which appeared in AESCULAPE, Number 4, April, 1925, the official organ of the *Societé Internationale d'Histoire de la Médecine,* Paris.

nineteen, the Academy of Padua entrusted to him the chair of logic and philosophy. For seven years, Fracastoro occupied this chair in a brilliant manner, and when the war which ravaged Italy had scattered his students and when through the death of his father he was deprived of support, he found a protector in General Alviano in charge of Venetian troops, and, through him, became one of the first masters of the Academy of Porto-Naone.

After the death of Alviano, Fracastoro returned to Verona which he had barely quitted, bringing with him from Porto-Naone the rough draft of a poem, which would be published in 1530 and which would serve to illuminate his name. This was none other than the poem entitled: SYPHILIDIS SIVE DE MORBO GALLICO LIBRI TRES.

According to modern taste, it seems a strange thing to sing of syphilis in three books; but one must judge all things according to their times. At that time no opprobrium was attached to syphilis, and no notices concerning the disease were affixed to the walls of public urinals. Had not the good priest, Francisco Delgado caught it? Without any attempt to conceal the fact, he had written a book to inform the world how he had been cured of the malady and this treatise on the various methods of curing the pox had appeared in 1529 under pontifical privilege.

On the other hand, if it were shocking to put into verse the judicial institutions of Justinian, as certain moderns have done for our civil code, it was not out of the way to mix poetry and medicine, for were not both, the daughters of Apollo?

In prosody, Giovanni di Milano, among others, wrote the thousand verses of his SCHOOL OF SALERNO, *and as far as syphilis itself was concerned, the Castilian, Francisco de Villalobos composed in 1498, his treatise concerning the*

xiv

pestiferous buboes. Nor am I far from thinking that this little work was known to Fracastoro. Although it is very different from his SYPHILIAD, *the two writers meet on common ground in their enthusiasm for a mercurial treatment and in the belief in the astrological origin of the malady which was world wide at that time. The rest is of no importance.*

For this work, Girolamo chose a poetic form, and, thereby literature has gained a poem that is by no means valueless and medicine has lost nothing.

In regard to the first statement, Haller, whom Mr. Alfred Fournier has followed, is of another opinion. But this is a matter of appreciation, and matters of taste cannot be discussed. Nevertheless, when I note how the humanists of the renaissance valued their contemporaries, nor were loath to praise them; when I note that such a man as Sannazaro, who had taken twenty years to compose his poem, held Fracastoro's work in greater esteem than his own, I am somewhat reverent. And I admire freely the powerful imagination of the faultless composition, when I read the pages that tell of the death of Torriani and depict at the same time the misfortunes of Italy.

From the medical point of view, Fracastoro saw indeed that the affection was of a contagious nature and that it was an infection of the blood particularly harmful to man.

He observed that the union of the sexes was a common cause of the disease and that a suckling could contract the malady from an infected wet-nurse, or give it to her, if he happened to have the disease. He stresses but little the primary symptoms, but shows that he is acquainted with the long period of incubation that precedes the secondary symptoms, which he knows how to describe well. Nor has the teritiary stage escaped him.

He mentions the cutaneous manifestations of the in-fection, and above all, the serious pustulary and scabby forms. Also he mentions the falling of the hair, the syphi-litic lesions of the palate, pharynx and eyes. He notes the inflammation of the bones and bone tumors, the localized nocturnal pains so often periarterial, the enemia, the gen-eral debility accompanied by slight fever, the syphilitic cachexia, and as all agree, he traces with a masterly hand, a picture, which, if it be not perfect in every particular, is at least rich in documentation, and one that may be con-sulted with benefit.

Beside the SYPHILIAD, our Veronese published a num-ber of valuable works. Among them should be mentioned in particular, his DE CONTAGIONIBUS ET CONTAGIOSIS MOR-BIS ET EARUM CURATIONE LIBRI TRES, which appeared in 1546 and which was exact in its treatment of venereal dis-eases. Freed from the exigencies of form, this prose work gives Fracastoro's medical ideas which are the least obsolete.

As for the rest, one is tempted to remain silent concern-ing his pathogenic theories and also the treatments that he advises. The heavy dust of oblivion falls on his ideas which are four centuries old and like to columns that stand when the palaces they have supported have been razed.

According to the theories of Fracastoro, and not unlike those of our day, one person infects another with the malady. The contagion is passed by means of a specific agent, infinitely small and thus escaping our detection. This agent is called the germ of contagion or virus by Fracas-toro, the microbes that the microscope has revealed to us of today, save in the case of a filter-passing virus of which we are still ignorant.

Furthermore, the therapeutics of Fracastoro is not to be despised. He was careful in his attempt to hinder the entry of infectious germs into the human organism, and is not this very similar to our prophylaxis? Then, if the precautions were in vain, he advised, when possible that the germs should be attacked and destroyed.

It is true that the desire to achieve and the choice of means by which we achieve are two very different things. Many things that the Veronese physician advocated are no longer held in esteem. The numerous vegetable remedies which he used, seem to us to be without specific virtue. The guaiacum which he preferred to mercury has been abandoned, and, for a little, we have failed the nymph, Lipara.

Everything is not exact in the work of the syphilographer Fracastoro, and often very indefinite, but what remains definite in this world? Not even the work of men, deceased barely yesterday. Of the work of the Veronese physician, there remains at least his poem, and fate, just for once, accorded him the honor of giving to syphilis, the name of the shepherd he sang, in place of the many names borne in turn by the malady.

Nevertheless, it is an error to think that all of the work of Fracastoro lies there. His writings, I repeat, were numerous, touching upon a number of fields, and if I have not mentioned them, it is not through disdain, but because I must be brief.

Fracastoro's contemporaries were not unmindful of the value of his writings and in 1545, when it was necessary to choose a chief physician for the Council of Trent, Pope Paul III made him archiater, and no one contested the choice of the Veronese savant.

In book four of his HISTORIA MEI TEMPORIS, Jacques Auguste de Thou, in telling us of this matter, says that the Pontiff defied the cardinals who worked for Charles V,

*and sought to bring the Council to papal territory. Fracas-
toro, physician and astrologer, intervened to bring this
about. Consulting the stars, he did not fail to read therefrom the presage of an approaching pest that would deci-
mate the City of Trent in particular. The delegates fled in
fright. The truth is simple. In all probability some little
known contagious malady was raging in the town at the
time, and the chief physician had merely to speak of it
publicly in order to transfer the Council to Bologna which
was done.*

*This was the last official act in the life of Fracastoro.
When the interminable CHAPITRE PUERIL DES LANTERNES,
as Rabelais called it, returned to Trent in 1550, the archiater was sixty-seven years of age. Retiring to his country
home at Incassi, Fracastoro occupied himself with poetry
and wrote his epic poem entitled JOSEPH. Then Death
passed, and he was brutal. On the eighth of August, 1553,
the poet was felled by an apoplexy.*

*His body was borne to Verona where it was interred
with great pomp in the Church of Saint Euphemia. In
remembrance of him, Padua placed his effigy in bronze in
the cloister of the Benedictines. Six years later, Verona
raised a marble statue to him.*

ALBERT GARRIGUES.

TRANSLATOR'S INTRODUCTION

TRANSLATOR'S INTRODUCTION

HE READER *may wonder why one takes the trouble to translate Fracastoro's* SYPHILIAD. *It is primarily intended for physicians, but the physician of today is too busy a man to labor with its original hexameters, even though he were inclined to do so, and the lay reader will find less incentive to read them.*

In recent years there has been too great a tendency to become interested in little else than human documentation. Since Freud has been clasped to the public bosom, we have had a literature of intimacies. For example, in one of the early scenes of BABBITT, *we find that worthy playing with the hairs on his shins as he sits in a matutinal bathtub, and* LADY CHATTERLY'S LOVER *takes even more intimate liberties, and modern writers boggle at nothing.*

The day of objective writing seems to be over for the time being at least. This is partially due to the absurdities that were introduced into the mid-Victorian romances whose women were creatures of syncope and whose men were in the main, lady-like. At that period the romancers gave us such underdone characters as ROCHESTER *and such overdone characters as* SIR MULBERRY HAWK, *both of these non-human humans being a departure from truth that is so infuriating in its inanity, that both writers and a reading public have turned away not unnaturally from such milk-and-water figments of the imagination and have sought relief in intimacies of a more or less revolting kind such as the condition of one's temper, due to sexual repressions, or the condition of one's genito-urinary tract, due to the same reason.*   **XX**

Today, we have wandered so far from Fracastoro, that it is refreshing to return to him. It must be borne in mind that when he wrote his SYPHILIAD, the FRENCH DISEASE (Italian, German, Spanish, Christian, Polish, according to one's location) was subject to no opprobrium, and that it was considered to be as devoid of sin as whooping-cough.

Had it been written to-day, it would have found difficulty in obtaining a publisher, and as far as obtaining fame for its author, it would have gone scarcely beyond a printer's devil. But in spite of this, the SYPHILIAD remains a valuable contribution to belles-lettres. That a successful sixteenth century physician could write polished Latin verses that compare favorably with those of Virgil, speaks volumes for the culture of his day.

The favorable reception of this poem was instantaneous. Sannazaro, the most accomplished Latin poet of the day, went so far as to say that he considered Fracastoro's hexameters superior to his own that had taken twenty years to compose. Such a generosity of spirit can find no counterpart among the writers of today. At that particular era men were more interested in what they did than in themselves. At that time, the ferocious individualism of a writer that prevails today, was not in vogue. Creative literature as we know it had not come into being, and no first class writer scorned the rewriting of a twice-told tale.

The values of the SYPHILIAD were many. Then, human beings were eager to learn as much as possible about this new disease that tore at them so ruthlessly. Here was a new enemy as devasting as tuberculosis and as malign as leprosy. Nothing was known concerning the disease and even its origin was a matter of conjecture.

Fracastoro was peculiarly fitted to write of the malady. As a practicing physician he had had much experience with it, and was he not one of the foremost scholars of Italy? Had he not taught philosophy at "Il Bo," at the tender age of nineteen? Had he not added to the sciences of mathematics, botany, and astronomy at an age when most men were considering the choice of a profession? Had he not proved himself to be a writer of no mean ability? Gifted with a fertile imagination, this good physician was a man among men to treat of such a subject. And this poem was hailed with delight by his contemporaries.

But what of us of today? Primarily the physician will be interested to find out just how much this Veronese knew of a malady that has flailed the world for nearly five centuries. And he will find that Fracastoro's knowledge was not slight in regard to the symptoms and the progress of the disease.

Furthermore, he will find that if Fracastoro is wrong scientifically in the parlance of today, he is by no means wrong in the scientific jargon of his own day. Astrology was budding into astronomy and alchemy was blossoming into chemistry. There was a refreshing faith in the simples. To his contemporaries there is no unsophistication in the fact that the cause of the malady was ascribed to the syzygy of Mars, Jupiter and Saturn. This was to be accepted as seriously in 1530 as Schaudinn's SPIROCHAETA PALLIDA was to be accepted in 1905. What the scientists of that day believed, they believed as firmly as that which the scientists of today believe, and, perhaps more firmly, for scientific theories change with a greater rapidity now than they did then.

It is less than thirty years since the spirochaeta of syphilis was discovered, and it is less than seventy years since Pasteur gave us the theory of bacteria as disease producers. Fracastoro believed that invisible particles were the cause of the various maladies. What he did not know was that these minute particles were ALIVE. *Yet he was very close to the truth.*

W. V. W.

Saint-Cloud, Seine et Oise,
August 1, 1933.

BOOK ONE

Within the purple womb of night, a slave,
The strangest plague returned to sear the world.
Infecting Europe's breast, the scourge was hurled
From Lybian cities to the Black Sea's wave.
When warring France would march on Italy,[1]
It took her name. I consecrate my rhymes
To this unbidden guest of twenty climes,
Although unwelcomed, and eternally.

What congress of an influence occult
Delivers this steely era to insult?
I sing victorious man and his intent;
I sing his genius, when he would recourse
To wit of gods, heroic expedient
To take this ill and trace it to its source.
I would interrogate the very air,
The shooting stars that sweep about the sky.
I would discover some newer thoroughfare
That leads to this uncharted sea, and I

---

[1] In 1494, Charles VIII sent an expeditionary force into Italy in order to support his claim to the throne of Naples. It was shortly after this that syphilis spread through Europe.

The following names were given to the disease at first, to-wit: *las bubas, morbus pustularm* (Spain); *lo male de le tavelle* (Genoa); *il male delle bole* (Florence); *lo male de le brossule* (Milan); the French disease (Naples); the Neapolitan evil (France); the French pox and the Bordeaux evil (Germany and England); the Spanish pox (Holland and North Africa); the Castilian disease (Portugal); the Christian disease (Persia); the Polish disease (Russia); the German disease (Poland).

It is interesting to note, in this general evasion of responsibility, how each nation attempted to blame the other for the malady, and how eager were all the nations in their acceptance of Fracastoro's name for the disease.

Would ask the Muses, a so-learned band,
That flower-strewn be my path at their command.

O Cardinal, the Light of Italy,[2]
Let Leo pause to turn his mighty brain[3]
From guidance of this Christian world that he
Alone has the dominion to maintain!
To my voice let him turn a willing ear.
Bembo, it bears the fruit of vigils long.
Torch of the Universe, so without fear,
Phoebus-Apollo loved the art of song!
Frivolous things have interests that abide.
My painting is a so-weak veil to hide
Nature's own laws and happy mysteries
And Fate, the maker of their least decrees.

And you, O Compass of their measured road,
On heavens' vault let myriad fires be sowed,
Sweet Charioteer of such celestial fire,
Guiding the floating spheres' harmonious choir!
Show me, Uranus, every secret cause
That rules our lot and makes a planet's laws,
And climates, years and seasons everywhere
And unseen poisons filling all the air.

[2] Piero Bembo, the cardinal to whom Fracastoro dedicated this poem, was greatly appreciated as a writer in his day. His most highly esteemed work is a history of Venice, written in Latin.
[3] Pope Leo X was the son of Lorenzo the Magnificent and Clarice Orsini. Before his elevation to the Holy See, he had been Cardinal Giovanni de' Medici.

Unto this humid shade must you descend,
O Muse, to give me both the means and end
That nature bids me sing! A sportive breeze
And murmuring plays amidst these myrtle-trees,
Stirring Benacus' and its clamorous waves,
Re-echoing in its deep, eroded caves.

O Muse, reveal to me what seed has grown
This evil that for long remained unknown!
Till Spanish sailors made the west their goal,
And ploughed the seas to find another pole,
Adding to this world a new universe.
Did these men bring to us this latent curse?
In every place beneath a clamorous sky,
There bursts spontaneously this frightful pest.
Few peoples has it failed to scarify,
Since commerce introduced it from the west.
Hiding its origin, this evil thing
Sprawls over Europe, just as shepherds bring
(When sparks fall from their illy lighted torches)
To stubble the slow gait of creeping fire,
Fanned by a wandering breeze until it scorches
The fields and mighty flames make them a pyre,
Conquering highland, lowland and the vale,
And spreading over all a blazing trail,
Till forests fall that once were thick and proud,
And all the countryside becomes a shroud

' Now Lago di Garda.

Of blackened wastes both sinister and drear,
When lulled to sleep has been their lurid glow.

This pestilence's savage voice I hear,
And wandering to our houses, will it sow
In tender virgin breasts a wicked seed,
Hatched from a poison that no vice has wrought.'
And from its evil clutches none is freed.
It is at home in hovel and the court,
Its symptoms never twice the same, indeed.
This plague's so ruthless hand's in every place,
And ever striking at the human race;
Rome has it from the mountains to the sea
And it is found within twin Sicily.
Ausonia' has it. In the fields it's seen,
And where the Sagra twists in patterns green.
The hundred cities that the Tiber laves
Caught it and also Po's so-tranquil waves
Which, swollen by a hundred rivers' gift,
Rush to the sea in undulations swift.
And, everywhere, a single voice's sigh
Mounts heavenwards in a so distracted cry,
The cry of those who fear the swerveless wrath
Of this fell evil on its ruthless path,
Sparing no blow until a plague will find
The furtherest border, borne on every wind.

' Fracastoro believed that syphilis might be transmitted without contact.
' A Greek term for Latium and Campagnia, and one of many synonyms for Italy employed by the Augustan poets.

The Spanish sailors, proud as they could be,
Challenged a vast and an uncharted sea.
Were they the vanguard of this suffering?
And Italy and France soon felt the sting
Of this new horror. In its dreadful sweep,
It caught all sailors tossing on the deep.
Soon the Palatinate and all its folk
And northern climates in their garb of snow,
The plague invaded at a single stroke,
For everywhere the scourge was swift to go.
A ruined Carthage felt its mighty sway.
The Nile, with its abundant wealth and free,
Flooding its banks with gifts, soon felt the teen
That overcame its vast prosperity.
And Idumea,' with its golden sheen
Of desert, with its fruits and palms so green,
Found all too soon this violent, awful curse
So newly hatched throughout the universe,
Evading every common rule. I pause,
Before I link this ill with Nature's laws
And drag therefrom the sadly curious truth
Of this wild blight that has no slightest ruth.

Are not all creatures, be they of the soil,
Or of they air, to streak a rapid flight,
Or of the sea's transparancies a-boil,
Beneath Fate's laws, or be they wrong or right?

' Idumea is the biblical Edom which is near the Dead Sea.

The simple and the complex spring to light,
Flooding the air and sea and all the earth,
Of different qualities and different worth.

That they be born, time, circumstance and place
Have all conspired that Fate's fell embryo
Lies in the womb of night a weakening space.
The strength of centuries will it forego,
And germinates in spite of this to grow,
And follows men with evil steps, at length
In origin as different as in strength.

On elephant-legs' Ausonia may smile,
Knowing them not. And lichen' has its sway
Upon the burning banks cooled by the Nile.
This subtle poison also has a way
Like unto these. Torn from the light of day,
'Twas plunged in darkness. And how numberless
Its victims now and dire is their distress!

It's ageless, though it hasn't any name,
Being forgotten by the human race.
And, finally, unrecognized it came,

---

[8] At the time that Fracastoro was writing this passage, elephantiasis was
endemic in Egypt and Arabia. There was also a species of the malady in
Greece. The Arabian elephantiasis is somewhat similar to the West Indian.
The Grecian species resembles neither.
[9] Lichen appeared in Italy during the reign of Claudian. Invading Illyria
(now the Dalamtian coast), it entered France and Italy.
  Pliny mentions it and tells us that it left hideous scars upon the counten-
ances of its victims.

The rear-guard of Time's march. Time can efface
So many things. Tell me, what son may trace
His forebears, and for Time's erasing hands?
Oceanward went this evil toward new lands.

Ever is it contagious and one sees
It born for common woe. And it appears
Everywhere with such strange diversities,
Changing in every climate through the years.
Atlantis-fruit, it adds to human fears.
The womb of centuries has given it birth.
Go, curious mortals, go and seek its worth!
Attempt to seize this all mysterious force.
Explore the surface of the globe, where dwell
All humans stricken in this plague's mad course,
Tracing its origin to heaven or hell.
Alas, is not this ill too prompt to fell
(Quicker than lightning) people everywhere?
Find its source in the water, fire, or air!

Is it of air, whose each unhealthy wave
Weighs on the body, every breast to lave,
Wherever Nature's atmospheres will spill,
First cause of all calamities that kill?
Creator-Principle of all the living
Is the air, pregnant with its ferments, giving
Corruptions to its fluid mass and, spent,
Striking at humans with vile intent.

Learn how the air gives people each disease,
Air, the invincible for centuries.

Numberless planets, ruled by the sun,[10]
Interpret the heavens' wishes, and with ease;
Governing earthly troubles, every one,
Shaking the land, the air, and even seas.
Are not the scattered stars of heaven's tent
Pathfinders for a new and serried way?
Submitting to them, every element
Bows to the changes underneath their sway.

Lord Phoebus rules the winter solstice, so
Toward the South Pole his chariot must go,
When he casts slanting glances at our sphere.
Then skies are darkened by thick fogs and drear
And snows bind soil beneath a blanketing,
And leafless trees with ice are glittering,
And rivers, frozen from their mouths to sources,
Stop in their icy and immobile courses.

Later when Cancer rules the heated land,
Phoebus has fiery floods at his command
That burn our fallows, withering our fields,
Until the forest shade and freshness yields
And grass goes tawny and Dame Nature must

---

[10] To sixteenth century physicians who believed in astrology, the Zodiac played an important part both in therapeutics and diagnosis. Each sign of the Zodiac ruled over certain parts of the human body.

Find her bright beauty dimmed by clouds of dust.

Phoebe, the Moon, whose disc, unlike the day's,
Illuminates the night with silvery rays,
Holds both the sea and every humid place
Beneath her rule, the whiles she drifts through space
To penetrate all bodies. Sinister
Saturn will glance awry. Jove, we infer,
Would be propitious. Venus and Mars the dire,
Against all humans, planets would conspire.
Elements waiver 'neath their fell empire,
When they converge at some spot in the skies,
Mingling their courses and their auguries.

Inverted in their normal march, will they
Seek for new orbits on a heavenly way.
So many a time, beneath the summer's heat,
This season brings disaster rushing fleet.
And every planet from great Jove to Mars
Governs our fate and to the whirl of stars,
Whose tread is sure for all their ponderous ways.
The Fates, alas, determine all our days!

Now an event, enchained from age to age,
Shakes off its shackles, frees itself at last.
The fatal hour has struck. Ills that were fast
Are freed, and air and water in their rage
Would they invade, and all the land as well.

The skies go grey. Compressed, the cloudlets swell
To vomit all their torrents on the air.
Rivers have thrust them from high summits bare,
To smash the trees to pieces in their wrath,
And sweep the fields. Released from their banks' path,
They kill the flocks within the rocky fold.
The Po superb, impetuous Ganges bold,
Thrust them beyond their waves' tumultuous bed,
Swallowing every house. Thus, ruin is spread
And hills are shattered, woods submerged in places,
And the immensity of flooded spaces
Makes them seem oceans under Neptune's keeping.
With skies afire, the water-nymphs a-weeping,
Watching their habitat evaporate.
Winds in their might have come to devastate
The world anew, and all their rage will be
Doubling this horror of calamity.

Hurricanes shake earth to its very heart.
Cities and walls and towers fall apart.
Alas, a day of wrath will come to be
Cursed by the gods and for their jealousy!
The land, with bounteous vegetation spread,
Will drown or languish uninhabited,
And suns will seek new paths for unknown reasons
And change the very cycles of the seasons.
Unusual heat or unexpected cold
Will swerve the orbits foreordained of old.

New lands will form beneath still newer skies,
And harmless beasts and those of cruelties
And races born of chaos will take their course,
Drawing their lives from some supernal source.
And no man, in the pride of this rebirth
Of the old fossil bones of Mother Earth,
Gives thought to Enceladus and his crew;[11]
To Typhon,[12] hundred armed giant, who
Piled Pelion on Ossa that he scale
Olympus' height, or so runs Homer's tale.

And if this fatal future will reveal
Itself, air hides within its bitter breast
Unknown and evil ferments against weal
To pour on people who are much distressed,
Condemned to plagues and poisons which may be
Discerned in signs of fresh calamity.

Two centuries before this, in the skies,
Saturn and Mars would lock their silent cars.[13]
All who were born beneath Dawn's witcheries,
On Ganges' plains, beyond the realm of Mars,
Found fever bursting forth to sweep the earth,

---

[11] Enceladus, son of Tartarus and Ge (Earth), made war on the gods. Killed by Zeus, he was buried under Mount Aetna.

[12] Typhon was a monster of a hundred heads. He fought against the gods and was subdued by Zeus. He was the father of the non-beneficial winds and of the Harpies. In his war on the gods, and with the other giants, he attempted to pile Pelion on Ossa which in turn were to be piled on Olympus in order that heaven might be scaled.

[13] The black death of the fourteenth century was supposed to have been due to the syzygy of Mars and Saturn.

Pouring on frightened folk its seething flood.
Then, breathless lungs and arid throat gave birth
To foetid and to black and yellow blood
That gained in strength before each falling breath
That four days later led a man to death.
Assyria and Persia felt its force,
And the Euphrates on its sluggish course;
A Tigris underneath its balmy sky,
And Egypt and Arabia, by and by,
Knew the fell urge of this so-vile disease
That snatched at Europe, reaching overseas.

Unto the gods' abode now lift your eyes
With me to contemplate those airy places
Where whirlwinds form that tear away the skies
And planets plough their divers way through spaces.
Kindly examine now their fell conjunctions,
Foretelling evil omens. And their functions
Have not the skies ordained and for our fears,
The destinies that menace all our years?
Perchance they will unveil themselves and bare
Sources of ill that strikes us everywhere.

Observe the Crab. It opens its great claws
Which would defend Olympus in their jaws.
Perfidious sign of an all sinister fire
Will it predict an evil fell and dire.
The great stars on their vagabondish way

Would join the Crab. These menace in their day
A world, to write in their conspiring flame,
How one Sirinis[14] with Uranus came
Unto Olympus, and, inspired and old,
His voice, prophetic for its auguries,
Cried out: "Fell gods," (he dared to make so bold)
"What floods of evil pass before mine eyes!
Upon these plains, I see the very air
Carry the seeds of poison everywhere.
Combats and wars of great impiety
(Involving all of Europe too) I see.
O land of Latins, all your fecund plains
Are smothered in your blood, and naught remains!"
Thus speaking, with an aged, trembling hand
He drew this desolation of our land.

Reaching the zenith of a heavenly way,
The sun has measured to the centuries
Those hours that rule the fate of earth and skies,
Under the king of gods' eternal sway.
An era of calamity restored,
Jupiter calls a congress of the stars,
Evoking Saturn and the war-god Mars,[15]

---

[14] Sirinis seems to be a fictitious character invented by the author in order that he may utter a prophecy that has no basis in classical mythology. This expedient was often resorted to by fifteenth and sixteenth century writers.

[15] Among other fourteenth century writers, the famous surgeon, Guy de Chauliac (c 1325-1368) attributed the black death to the conjunction of Saturn and Mars and Jupiter which took place on March 22, 1345 in the fourteenth degree of Aquarius.

Fracastoro attributes the epidemic of syphilis to the syzygy of the same planets in the sign of Cancer.

Asking their aid and as their overlord.
That he ordain the future's course, he calls
The Crab, the guardian of the sacred walls,
To open the double doors of heaven's halls.

There the immortals sit. The very first,
Crowned with a sanguine crest where lightnings burst,
Is Mars the ravager and warrior. He
Holds all the carnage of the victory.
Jupiter follows in a car of gold,
Being for peace and filled with equity,
Unless the Fates shall bind his clemency.
Then Saturn, scythe in hand, advances. Old
Is the man for the fardels of the years.
He treads a palsied path, his many fears
And hatreds in his heart caused by his son
Whose insults make him brood. This ancient one
Submits with difficulty to Jove's will,
A thousand detours rendering his route ill
Decided. Far too halting is his path.
Oppressing him (he scarce can hide his wrath)
Are sterile threats. He mutters endlessly.
Jove on his throne is ill at ease and he
Weighs with reluctant hands the misery
The Fates ask for the world. A futile plea
Makes this god groan. Ever reserve the Fates
Ills and reverses both for folk and states.
And death and fire will tear the universe.

And this new, raging torment Jove would curse.
When gods decree, Olympus too is riven,
And to the air is this new poison given,
By aerial ways sent over spaces wide.
Here's the effluvium of homicide.
And north and south from sunset to sun's rise,
And scattered by the wings of night, it flies.
For the sun's rays, the earth is withered too,
And stars would send their flaming toxins through
The power of their concentrated rays,
That earth be tainted in a thousand ways.
Oceans exhale misasmic miseries
Carried upon the air as well as seas.
Mixing with these new evils and unseen,
Poisons cooperate, on mischief bent,
Contagions following where they have been,
Changing the atmosphere to some extent.

Let me not hide, for all my halting speech,[16]
The difficulties crowding me. For each,
I ask that heaven will link it to those things
That cause it. But a tardy heaven brings
Naught save delay. And, making no advance,
I find that this hangs on the play of chance,
Renewing endlessly mine every doubt,
Scattering many errors on my route.

---

[16] Here speaks a true scientist who would rid himself of the shackles of a superstitious astrology, one who is earnestly endeavoring to find the cause of the new malady.

Secretive in design, like nature too,
These varying poisons fill our earth with gloom,
Even innoculating trees in bloom,
Ravishing riant-crowned flowers. Steeped in rue,
They strip from blackened stubble every grain,
Till hope of harvest is destroyed again,
Although the sun is hot and skies are blue.
Their rage will spread to animals who die
When stricken. Only recently have I
Been witness to their all-erratic blows.
When a damp, soft and rainy southwind goes
Blowing a-down the coolth of autumn days,
Suddenly bursts this plague of evil ways
Upon the goats to kill them. First these went
Over the barriers of their pens, each bent
On pleasure. How they gambolled ere they died
Upon the neighboring pastures lush and wide!
The herdsmen who were lying in the shade
Upon their oaten reeds their pastorals played
To herds about them. Suddenly a goat,
Much shaken by a cough's devouring pain
Tearing so wildly at a panting throat,
Whirls madly. But its efforts are in vain.
It whirls and whirls that it may banish death.
After its dance, it gives its final breath,
Falling 'midst sisters frightened by its fall,
The first to answer bleak death's ruthless call.

The spring that followed and the summer's haze
Found minor cattle in the evil's maze.
Upon them this vile plague forever preyed
And heaven revealled itself and thus displayed
Its occult influence to change its course,
Cause and effect affected by its force.
Eyes' mobile veils would guard the eyes less well.
Nor can the lungs find shelter from the knell
Of this contagion of the foetid breath
That has become a messenger of death
To breasts and apple-trees where vines enlace
Their withered branches with a garland's grace.
Nothing escapes this evil's fires that burn,
And grains ferment and perish in their turn,
And wave no more for undulating wind.
A vanished sap and every pore awry,
Too open or too closed, have made them die.

Its form and seed will vary everywhere,
Knowing no bounds and limits, peoples, states.
Piercing time's night, it flashes through the air,
And, lightning-swift to strike, it contemplates ,
Hiding its origin within the skies,
Confounding all who would examine it.
The mute fish on the breast of ocean dies,
And every flock and divers birds are hit.
Cattle and sheep and coursers of the plain,
The wanderers that in the woods remain

Bear the contagion far and wide and yield
To man, who is a very fruitful field,
The poison that battens on him and to his bane,
So clotting blood attests in rotting vein,
Creeping along too sluggish and too fat,
When for the virus man's a blood-thickened vat,
In fearful mysteries these poisons blent
To bring to man adulterous ferment.

Let us make haste. 'Tis time I comb in verse
The symptoms and the aspects of this curse.
But can Apollo, who has fettered day,
Guide my slow footsteps to that Pierian spring
That Pegasus sought ere he had taken wing?
Let him diffuse fecundity in me
That I bear truth unto posterity.
And will my nephews use what I have said
To solve the sweep and nature of this plague?
Once conquered by oblivion and vague,
For long it lay enslaved and well nigh dead,
Only to plunge upon a new career,
Shaking the dust of many centuries,
Invading earth and air and skies and seas,
Borne by capricious Fates unto this sphere.
Will destiny revive its noxious rage,
To fell the peoples of another age?

The epidemic bursting, very soon,

Shutting her disc four times, a frightened moon
Showed by the signs that she would manifest
That this new evil would become a pest.
Within the body, long its ferment rests,
To nourish at some hidden source of breasts.
Then suddenly, beneath a langor's weight,
The victim creeps about in fearful state,
The heart defective and the slightest strain
Tiring the limbs, while energies remain
All sapped. A gloomy eye and saddened face
Of sickly pallor bend to this disgrace,
And soon a vicious ulcer eats its way
Into the privates. And a vengeful sway
Takes cancerous possession to remain.
Extended to the groin is its fell bane.

Gone is the sheen of day that was so bright,
Abandoning the earth to shades of night.
At dusk the body's innate heat is sent
To every organ, till it's weak and spent.
The impure ferments rushing at their will
Spread a wild torture, fever and a chill.
Shoulders and legs and arms shake madly too,
And for the irritation passing through
The veins, the poisons being all-obstructing,
An agent both corrosive and corrupting.

Soon is the body ulcerous and vile.

VENUS
Belegert en Ontset.
Ofte Verhandelinge van de
POKKEN
en der selfs
TOEVALLEN

t'AMSTERDAM
Gedrukt, by Timotheus ten Hoorn, Boekverkoper, in de
Nes vast de Brolle Gront. 1696.

The face becomes within a little while
A mask of running pustules small and great.
A horny shell will glands well imitate.
Breaking and emptying an acrid humor,
From pus-corroded skin, pours every tumor.
And bloody ulcers deeply dig away,
Gnawing the tissues that they make their prey.
Then is man stripped until his piteous moans
Come from a skeleton of putrid bones.
The lips are torn to shreds for this vile ill,
And, ere the voice dies, it is harsh and shrill.

Vigilant nature would attempt to pass
The poison out, but this so-noxious mass
Resists her gentle power and so kind.
Viscous and obstinate and slow to bind,
The poisons torture dermis in a tussle,
Attacking joints and bones and even muscle,
Leaving upon the skin an ill infecting,
And ever all too subtle, and collecting
On the extremities, and here one sees
A hundred symbols of this dread disease.

By Iseo's lake, where Oglio's river flows,
Confined of wave, enriching for its part
Fat pasture-lands, through Mantuan fields it goes.
There an Ausonian hits me to the heart.
No noble youth more fortunate is born,

Crowned with the many buds of his spring's tide,
Illustrious of birth and of the morn,
Many seductive charms in him abide.
Rich is he and all glorious to behold.
Superb his arms are and his helm of gold.
And, loving well all manly sports, this boy
Is faster than the stag he holds at bay.
Ever meets he and with a mighty joy
The bear and boar upon a woodland way.
Nymphs of the fields and forests are nigh mad,
And Oglio's water-nymphs, for this fair lad.
For her desire for him, each nymph has yearned
To pleasure with him. How each one has burned,
Exposed to his contempt! To punish him,
One of them prays for vengeance. As a whim,
Too promptly all the high gods grant her this.
The whiles the lad sleeps by a deep abyss,
All innocent, without the slightest fear,
Nor recks of the contagion that is near.
And in his happiness he is so blind
He recks not of a future so unkind,
That gods bring to him, this fell malady.

Gone is the brilliance of his youth and spring.
Dying by inches, as his soul sinks, he
Finds on his limbs a hideous leprosy.
Upon his very bones would caries fling
Its banners, till they open to the eyes.

His lovely eyes that were so long alight—
Ulcers devour these—a hideous sight.
Purulent poison too his nose corrodes,
Until, for viscous humors, it explodes.
But not for long remains this sorry soul.
And asking for it, he receives death's goal
To end his sufferings and finds this sweet.
The Po and Oglio spill their tears and bring
Their nymphs to exile in a dark retreat.
They seek the shadows for their suffering.
The Alps, for sorrow, mingle sighs and groans
With Iseo's half-uttered, smothered moans.

Sinister Saturn's mighty influence,
Aloof from plagues, dispersed their seeds intense
And no less cruel, to shorten all our days.
Mars would cooperate with Saturn's ways,
And so the scourage was born, and for their rage;
The worst of all, the worst of any age,
Mounting from hell in all its darkling doom,
From Styx's cavern of eternal gloom,
And vomiting that it depopulate
The earth, to leave it in a frightful state.

O gods! Ausonia, given by your desire
To fate! O founder of Rome's vast empire,
Saturn, what crimes, committed by your race,
Have put the weight of such a vile disgrace

On Latium that it finds misfortune's bane?
Even those folk not yet exempt from pain
Why should an unjust heaven upon them pour
A rage and misery, not yet reached before,
Save by Parthenope?" Of regicide,
Of death of states, of pillage far and wide,
Let me depict some scenes. Carnage would gush
The blood of hosts who, wild for battle, rush
With equal ardor. France and Italy
Along the Taro's banks for spoils would be.
And how that stream's accelerated wave
Is seething seaward! Po-ward will it lave
Horses and men piled pell-mell, in a heap.
Swollen with blood, then later will it sweep
Toward the Adige's friendly bank to wend
Toward untamed Po that mourns a feckless friend.

See, a disorder's fruit within our land!
Unhappy Italy, your sceptre's torn
(That used to stretch as glorious as the morn,
For forebears) from your far too feeble hand .
Is there no corner of the globe still free
From outrage and where war has never shed
The people's blood, to bind in slavery
The conquered who aren't better than the dead?

" The Siren, Parthenope, cast herself into the sea because Ulysses refused
to listen to her song. Where her body was cast ashore by the waves, was
founded the city of Parthenope, later, New City (Neapolis), and today,
the City of Naples.

Answer, O noble land, whom conquest makes
Sorrowful! Hillsides fertile with fine grapes
The Adige bathes in new sterility,
Wandering in shamed detours to the sea.
Mine Italy, where is your ancient force?
Seaward your rivers take a slavish course.

Dear land, my land, that only yesterday
Hoped for the happiness of peace profound.
O soil of heroes! God's land! Holy ground,
Where is your ancient treasure? Torn away.
Your breasts, prodigious for Adige's flood,
Gave you fecundities so passing good.
Today, O Italy, what colors drear
Depict your suffering, your ills, your fear?
Trembling are all the strings of my poor lute
To tell of your misfortune, but are mute.
Garda, go hide your shame amidst your reeds.
Laurels no longer seek your waters' needs.

What a misfortune and alarm of strife
Have dried the very sources of our tears!
O victim of the Fates, a-down the years,
Beloved of Pallas, once with raptures rife,
Your hour has sounded! Noble Anthony[18]
Passes and naught can save you from the tomb,

---

[18] Marco Antonio della Torre was a Veronese physician who died at an
early age.

Still in the bloom of spring, O Italy!
Once nourished by the Muses, now by doom,
Sleep in the peace of Garda's banks to find
Amidst the rocks, her dripping waters fraught
With sobs, merely an echo left behind.
Adige mourns you, calling you, thus caught.
The mellow lyre of old Catullus' hand[19]
Might stir your woods again, O Fatherland!

Louis the Twelfth,[20] proud Genoa's fell bane,
Ravaged mine Italy to strike my heart.
And Maximillian[21] forged a mighty chain,
Enslaving Venice and to hold a part
Of the Udine. Latium mourns for this,
Finding her at the brink of an abyss.

[19] Gaius Valerius Catullus (87-57 B.C.), the Veronese Latin poet, borrowed much from Greece and from Alexandria. Fracastoro held his hexameters in very high esteem.
[20] Louis XII held a command in northern Italy under Charles VIII and he harried the Genoese in particular.
[21] Maximilian I (1459-1519) was a "gifted amateur in politics" and the disorders that he caused in Germany and Italy exposed him and the empire to the jeers of Europe.

BOOK TWO

Measuring the evil's strength and its extent,
I'll put the subject by a moment, so
That I tell of its habits. Mine intent
Is that I warn all men that they forego
This horrid poison. Let discoveries
Stop a world's loss because of this disease.

The menace of this plague seems limitless,
With scarce an opposition to its sway.
And its resources wax, to our distress,
If they be threatened on their evil way.
Efforts in Aesculapius' domain
Resulted in a glorious success,
When for this hydra, science forged a chain
To bind it and its so terrific bane.

Fate has created for us in new fields
Directions that our labors might be crowned.
Though many a fury the wild tempest yields,
Deliverance for us the gods have found.
Nor are the tenderest of azure skies
Forever closed to yearning, human eyes.
This century has seen the land war-glad,
And for this evil cities mourn the faster.
Kingdoms and thrones have toppled, being mad.
Penates seek the blood of their own master.
Altars and temples are defiled, dispersed,

Oceanica Classis

And many a river from its bank has burst
To catch our harvests and our forests too,
Scattering men and floods to spread, anew,
Cadavers over what was once the land,
Rendering sterile with unkindly hand.
Fallows are turned to deserts dry as dust.

Over the waves, sea-conquerors have thrust
Their prows to find immensities beyond
The sea of forebears, hardly more than pond.
When Poseidon's proud empire was thus ploughed,
Cape Verde became an unimportant goal;
Del Gado's Cape and Fortune's Isles less proud,[22]
All swept by storms assailing from the pole.
Zambezi's banks were found to be a rift,[23]
Kerman brought many an unexpected gift.[24]
Ganges and Indus soon were found to be
No universal limits. Men were free
To push beyond these barriers of the world,
Toward Phoebus and his morning flags unfurled.
China was won, and there, men at their leisure
Found ebony and many another treasure.
A god benign seemed all inclined to win
For hardy sailors new worlds not akin

---

[22] Capo del Gado is on the eastern coast of Africa. The Fortunate Isles
(insulas fortunatae) are the Canary Islands which have also been called the
Hesperides.
[23] Fracastoro calls the Zambezi, the Raptus.
[24] Kerman, which is a southeastern portion of Kabul, is called Yeman by
Fracastoro.

To ours. The seas were ploughed by starlight, so
By the Fornello's god,[25] all men might know
This hardiness for a new poet's voice
That made old Virgil's epic heart rejoice.
Virgil, the darling of the Muse, whose yield
Ennobled every wood and town and field,
Giving us with a brilliance, good and ill,
And for a mighty poet's noble will.

If Bembo, armed in his humility,
Will hide a name whose sheer ability
Renders it equal to the grandest name,
Let it escape me. Leo, Prince, whose fame
Is more than great, O precious gift, arise!
Honor of weeping earth and of the skies,
The Tiber murmurs to triumphant Rome
The mighty miracles that you bring to
The earth in places farthest from your home.
Even the stars, the most remote, know you.
Give to your land the blessed light of peace.
Illustrious omen, that all wars may cease.
Within our walls, a shelter from the blast,
The Muses settle, and your gentle voice
Gives Latium justice and wise laws at last,
Making the gods and very earth rejoice.[26]

---

[25] Fornello's god is the poet, Giacomo Sannazaro (1458-1530) called the Christian Virgil. He esteemed Fracastoro's poem as superior to his *De partu Virginis* which he took twenty years to compose; a generousness of point of view that is rare enough among writers of today.

[26] Leo X preached a crusade against the Turks, but without success.

You gave us war reluctantly, the while
Your name reverberated from the Nile
To the Euphrates and the Black Sea's crest,
As trembling waves lay fainting on its breast,
And the Aegean, flying from your reach
Hid all its shame and fear in halting speech.[27]

Others will celebrate your mighty sway,
Even the gracious Muses must give way
Before the burden of attempt, while waits
A watchful Bembo, as he consecrates
In an immortal book your wondrous fame.
My weakness importunes the very name
Of my more humble work, O man of men!
In fear and trembling, I take up my pen.

If nature has endowed your rushing blood
With qualities both pure and very good,
There's hope for you. Of that you may be sure.
If surging through your veins be blood impure
If body be thick with bile, in bloated state,
You may be certain that the danger's great,
Nor easily discovered is a cure.
Seek out the strongest remedies, nor fear
Fatigue, though it belabors somewhat drear.
And if you haste, success will crown your pains.

---

[27] Fracastoro refers here to the schism that occurred between the Roman Catholic and the Greek Orthodox churches.

Then is the plague less harsh within your veins.
Learn from the art of physic what to take.
Strangle the ill as though it were a snake
Newborn within its nest. Nor let it go.
The plague, too long within you, then may grow
To such proportions that it soon distresses
Its victim, and, invading him, oppresses.
Conquer by efforts of a savage kind
And ever must you keep this in your mind,
And see to it, engraved on memory,
Are the rules that assure a victory.

As for your habitation, it is plain
That you must shun the south wind and the rain.
Fly from foul marshes and damp, miry places,
And find the heights and open, fertile spaces.
Demand from hillsides sunshine and fresh air
And gentle breezes, rosy skies and fair.
And it is very well that you should be
Where north winds sweep the air incessantly.

Seek not repose, nor rest in lethargy.
As eager as a harrier, must you see
The bear and boar hunted upon the moor.[28]
Where summits lose themselves in white mists pure,
Follow some unknown footpath to a crest.

---

[28] One wonders why Fracastoro advocated such violent exercise for a malady that could never have supported it.

Rush through the woods and vales and never rest
Until the stag's at bay, when he would get
A shelter. Ever must you steam and sweat
Until the ill evaporates away.
Follow the plough and goad your oxen. Play
Them underneath the yoke until they plough
Rich furrows. And you never must allow
Idleness. Take a hoe and then belabor
Rapidly for yourself or for your neighbor,
With sweeping motions e'en a thankless soil,
For beneficial will you find such toil.
Sky-scraping oaks must axes overwhelm,
Though proud of branch, and every ancient elm,
Until great roots are scattered without ruth
Over the fields. Certes, and this is sooth.
Find you a house that yields but little rest.
The palm[29] is a sport that's good. Be not distressed
For all the struggle of this exercise.
See that your forehead's sweat will flood your eyes
To tame this ill. Be active with a zest,
No matter if fatigue advises rest.
Let the bed call in vain lest that you keep
A fatal calm, a too perfidious sleep.
Truce is a trap and all your efforts must
Reduce this mortal enemy to dust.
Be active if you wish to keep alive,

---

[29] *Jeu de paume* is a kind of tennis. Although *paume* means the palm of the hand, this game resembles handball in no way.

POVR VN
PLAISIR MIL
DOVLEVR
IL S'VE LA
VEROLLE

FOLIE   Il vaut mieux auoir plus de bourse
que de bouche.

Chaut comme
braise

Pourvn petit plaisir ie Souffre mille maux | Partout le Corps ie sue et ma machoir tremble
Ie fais contre vn Hyuer deux esté ce mesemble | Iene croy iamais voir la fin de mes trauaux

Or else the enemy may soon revive.

Look for a hearth and seek the ways of peace
And banish care with all its dangerous train
Of fears importunate. Let these in vain
Knock at your heart that you may have surcease
From wrath and hate and every gnawing thought.
Play-acting and the sportive dance are fraught
With some delight, and verse should hold a sway
As charmer so that cares may pass away.
Exile your mistress that a lonely bed
Shuns Venus and her altars and embraces.
And shun your love for all her tender graces,
Or for your lack of faith will she be dead.

Let me instruct you in your diet too,
Lest that your fardel be too hard to bear.
Of pool and lake-fish too you must beware.
Sea-fish and river-fish are not for you.
But if necessity demand you eat
Of fish, see that you have the lightest, mind,
And of a flesh so tender, white and sweet.
Swimmers on pebbly bottoms are the kind,
Or those who like to slide on troubled waves,
Or those who seek the bottom's many caves.
The gudgeon and the perch and not the gar.
Certes, and very good for you's the scar
Which (pilots tell us) ever likes to feed

(Skimming the waves) on succulent seaweed.

And here are more things, all forbidden too;
Assiduous hunters are the marsh-birds who
Seek in the stagnant waters for their prey.
Shun these, and ducks and geese as well, for they
Have blood too thick, especially the geese.
Since they saved Rome, why let them go in peace.
Allow the quail to migrate as he should.
Entrails and hams of hogs are never good.
Go, carry death to savage boars, but fast
And let no single one grace your repast.

Touch not the truffle or the artichoke.
Leeks and cucumbers leave to other folk.
And vinegar and milk you must let be.
For this will you be better off, and see
That your cup, smoking hot, contains no ichor
Of a full bodied wine or foaming liquor.
Falerno's and Pisano's sparkling wines
Are not for you, no matter what man dines
With you, or Corsica's when you would feast.
The Engadine's fine grapes may have the least
Of seeds, but generate a strength divine.
Fearlessly may you use some good light wine.
Spoleto offers one that to its lees
You may drink dangerless. The Naiades
Took out the sting that Bacchus had imparted

To it to make this liquor fiery-hearted.

Frugal in taste, and sage in every leaning
Toward food, the yield of fields must you be gleaning
Which burgeon gods' delight in sunny clime.
Go, find the bugloss, balm and mint and thyme[30]
That offer you salubrious surceases.
Certes, and ever better would you be,
Upon the mead, go seek the chicory.
Where fountains plash, the skirret too increases
The aid that winter's thistles tend to give.
The briar's pungent shoots will help you live.
The ladysmantle also brings you hope,
And thorny briars on a humid slope.
Ask that the hop will give you of its sprout.
Take briony wherever it spreads out
Its twisted branches on its thick old stalk.
Its clusters, when too much exposed, will balk,
Losing efficiency for evil juices.
And many other plants have varied uses.

---

[30] Mint was supposed to be good for the heart, brain and stomach. Bugloss purified the blood and excited joyfulness. Sium arrested dysentary.

Certainly this was the golden age of the therapeutic marvels of herbs. Both physicians and patients believed firmly that the simples were possessed of curative virtues.

In his work on syphilis, Cirillo goes so far as to state that oranges and lemons worked thousands of cures. Due to the fear of the new disease, heroic virtues were attributed to plants. Nor can one accuse the physicians of being quacks. The nature of the malady was such that many physicians may have been completely fooled by what seemed a cure, until further experience taught them not to be deceived by a period of quiesence.

There is something refreshing in Fracastoro's faith in herbs, a faith that may have removed many a mountain when dealing with a lesser infection than that caused by the *spirochaeta pallida*.

But since time limits me, I leave these, and
Proceed to other matters that command
My senses. Muses, in your lovely dell,
Open a way for me that I may tell
Of virgin woods where nature will await
Me with rewards for my vast work and great!
Reserve the laurel for me, for my years
Of labor, though I halt with many fears
For those I've striven to save, and, for my part,
True to the vows that justify my heart.
So let the oaken chaplet crown my hair,
For victims, once half-dead, who now are yare.

In spring or autumn, if these fell ills burst
Upon you, boiling veins may then be ripped
Asunder by your blood, till they be stripped
Of flesh. And for this evil, so accursed,
Your basilic and your median veins may be[31]
Aided by some new, drastic remedy
That will expel the poison, when the season
Will bring you every aid that is in reason,
Driving it from its dwelling, when in wrath
It will seek for another, newer path.
Let beverages bring you aid perforce,
That they defy the poison's bitter course.
And see that you (for this wild surge that tries

---

[31] The median vein is the superficial vein that passes up the middle of the front surface of the forearm, and the basilic vein lies along the inner border of the biceps muscle of the upper arm.

Your blood) search for Pamphylian remedies:
The Cretan thyme and fennel, celery-root,
The hop that grows in spirals, its green shoot,
The bitter sprout of lowly fumitory.
Let science learn from earth the treasured story
Of cures, and capillary's good humidity,
Of spleenwort's shame and its sterility.
Polypody upon its earthen bed,
And hartstongue with its leaf of brilliant red—
Extract the juices of these plants that you
Imbibe in drinking benefactions too,
So that the humors of this reeking mass
Of vile corruption may be slaked to pass.
If these prove fruitless, then without delay
Seek stronger agents that they go away.
Hellbore is good, and good are ginger's juices.
Cucumber and the squill have many uses.
Turpeth has active roots and they empower
This seaside plant to change its many a flower
Thrice daily, varying colors so intense.
Myrrh of Arabia and frankincense,
Lybia's gum and Nile's opopanax,
And scaly saffron and bedellium's wax
And fruit of the wild cucumber all yield
Surcease, a wealth of forest and of field.

Then, if your heart would freeze within your breast,
Fearing such puissant remedies; that you

May triumph over ravages that too
Harshly strike at your tottering form distressed,
Search for a gentler cure that by degrees
Will shockless take away your miseries.
Remember that upon a secret path
This ill moves, and dissimulating wrath,
Hiding its seed with caution and with care.
If from your body, you would snatch to-day
This ill. Rosin's propitious in its way.[32]
With it you may attack it anywhere.
Myrrh's tears and frankincense are without harm.
Cyperus has a perfume full of charm.
And palathus and cedar with its cone,
Aloes and sempervirens give new tone
To fight the evil. Cinnamon's a gem,
And bitter-cress and cassia on its stem
These may you find in humid field and marsh,
In sombre places that are chill and harsh.
Water-germander's virtue's good of course
To kill these poisons born of some foul source.
Its carriage, color, creeping vine and flowers
Are like the true germander's in their powers.
Gather its root and leaf when day is born,
When alliaceous odors still adorn
The plant. Then boil it in an earthen pot

---

[32] The claim to cure syphilis without resorting to mercurial treatment is almost as old as the disease itself. In Fracastoro's time, no aspersion of quackery was attached to the claim with justification, although this did not remain the case, unfortunately.

And drink it in deep draughts while it is hot.

Spain's ornament, the pride of Italy,
Think not my Muse forgets you, lemon-tree![33]
Others have praised you in far better rhyme.
Nevertheless, I'll consecrate some time
To you, if you will smile upon me, who
Am Epidauraus' son, immortal you.
Crowned with sweet branches that are ever green,
Upon your arms your endless blooms are seen,
Whose odors inundate the air. Your worth
And fardel of your fruit bend you toward earth.
O tree, beloved of Venus, soundlessly
This ill flows through men's veins in its wild rush,
Confined somewhat and somewhat boundlessly,
You are the very weapon that will crush
And kill it, you will take away our fears.
When for Adonis, Venus spilled her tears,
She shut within your golden rind a gift
Of heavenly virtues, energetic, swift.

Happily I've an idea for my part.
Look at this glass retort bent at the head,
With a straight neck and long! Its shape is spread,
Its sides are puffed, thus rounded by mine art
Of blowing it in fires so ardent red.

---

[33] It is natural that Fracastoro should wax poetic over the lemon-tree. Its leaves were used as a cordial, the rind overcame poisons that attacked the heart, stomach and brain. Its juice was good for blood and bilious disorders.

The ivy and marjoram odorific
Will it consume, till these be a specific
Mixture and vaporous. A humid stream
Will fill this globe with ever running steam,
For which this crystal prison is a snare
Of heat condensed and by the glacial air
Playing upon it, till a new form too
Of vapors is condensed to misty dew
Writhing and swirling in great spirals wide,
Confined until their waters pour outside
The glass. So, benefit by break of day
And drink this distillation right away,
Obtaining good warm clothing that you get
Yourself into a somewhat tardy sweat,
A simple, useful remedy that will
Strike at the subtle heart of this deep ill.

In tears and in convulsions for this thing,
Twisting for pain's implacable, harsh goad,
Liniments calm. And more benign your road,
When oil and wool-fat soothe somewhat its sting.
And limpid honey, pure and sweet and fresh,
Mixed with the fat of geese, their tenderest flesh,
And linseed paste and starwort well allied
With saffron and narcissus must be tied."

" Wool-fat has soothing properties. Narcissus bulbs are an emetic, and
saffron possesses this same quality.

Within the tissues' heart, a serpent-coil
Of ulcer is assuaged by this fine oil.
And copper nitrate will allay its creeping.[35]
Potassium's nitrate sends its bite to sleeping.
And when this ulcer sets a mordant tooth
Upon the throat, these follow without ruth
Upon the chancre's path and hold a sway.
And soon these caustics stop its grisly play,
Destroying every callous, and to boot,
Flaying the evil to its very root.

Soon is repaired the ruin of the flesh,
If lard be well applied that's good and fresh,
Or dyer's colors of a soothing power.
If some poor soul, impatient for the hour
Of sweet release, should find too slow this cure,
And yearning for a quicker and more sure,
Then stronger remedies without delay
Shall kill this hydra in another way.
For there are agents far more vigorous
Whose energies a profaned breast will thus
More rapidly allay its poisoned germ.
And with this kindling evil they'll be firm,
Though it's no easy thing to cure the pranks
Of this fell plague that tears away men's flanks.
These act as goad, their fires are ever burning.

---

[35] Causterization was destined to play a great role in the therapeutics of syphilis.

L'ESPAIGNOL
AFFLIGE
DV MAL
DE NAPLES

LE FRANCOIS · LE NAPOLITAIN · L'ESPAGNOL · LE TABLETER

Then comes a time when this ill will be turning
Away from all the tortures that it breeds.
Although a body be timid, still it cedes
Before these mighty unguents and intense.
Oxide of lead, mercury, frankincense,
Antimony and storax will provoke,[36]
If spread upon the flesh their caustic smoke,
Released to stop the progress of this ill,
And that they may attack with mighty will.
But there may be a source of wild regret,
If unsuccessful. Deeper driven yet
May be the ulcer on its biting path.
But I prescribe that these be used for all
The body if they mitigate at all
The harsh condition with its pain and pus
And rebel ulcers and tuberculous.

All men concede that mercury's the best
Of agents that will cure a tainted breast.
To heat and cold sensitive's mercury,[37]
Absorbing the fires of this vile leprosy
And all the body's flames by its sheer weight,

---

[36] Red oxide of lead was employed to dry ulcers. Storax was used as a stimulant and antimony was used to cause sweating.

[37] Mercury was known to the ancients as melted silver. It is the *arguron chuton* of Aristotle and the *argentum vivum* of Pliny, or quicksilver, quick which in its old sense means alive. It was considered a deadly poison and was prescribed as such and was introduced into the *materia medica* by the Arabs. Rhazes and Avicenna used it for skin eruptions such as scabies. Early in the history of syphilis it was used by Gilini and Torella in 1497, and by Benevinio and Hook in 1502 and by Angelo Bolognini in 1506. It ruled completely until Erlich discovered salvarsan.

Dissolving humors that it recreate
The health and with a fine, divided art
Applied to quench the flame right to its heart
And delving deep to every injured part.
Each acrid mollecule will in its turn
Seize upon every humor that will burn
The scourge away by secret energies
That hide from human eyes their destinies.

Pause for a moment, Muse, suspend your course
And tell what hand divine will show the source
Where all this precious, hidden metal lies.
And, for this boon, then let me thank the skies.
In what fair Syrian valley, in what glade
Of verdant willows and within what shade
Of sombre rocks, a sweet Callirrhoe[38]
Sends her nine jets in plashing radiancy?

Where murmurs in complaint each waving reed,
Here Ilseus cultivated, and were freed
The wood-gods. In this garden did he snare
The monsters of the forest everywhere,
Squandering the waves of this delicious spring
That unto odorous branches might he bring
Freshness, ere he was stricken by the flail

[38] As far as Fracastoro is concerned, Callirrhoe is more or less non-classical, for his sulphur-spring near Aetna has nothing to do with the celebrated well in Athens which is sometimes called Enneacrounos or the nine springs that had nine pipes for the distribution of its waters.

Of chance, to lie with forehead cold and pale,
Saying: "God of Thermalities whose hands
Calm every pain and close the open wound,
Callirrhoe, dear nymph, at whose commands
I've sacrificed (when hunting with the hound)
The mighty stag which often have I found
Within the wood, let me escape this ill
That stifles me. Then, kindly nymph and sweet,
I'll decorate your altar with a will,
Bringing the reddest fruits on tireless feet
To this abode so sweetly riant and
I'll hang them with appreciative hand,
Wedding the lily, hyacinth and rose,
Encircling this fair spot, as festoon grows
To garland's length." Then swooned he from the tiring
Effects of Phoebus' heat, nigh to expiring.

Hardby, within her cave, the limpid spring,
Gliding o'er moss and glossy rocks worn bare,
Callirrhoe heard his pathetic prayer,
And, wiping her damp locks, to him would bring,
As he lay on her breast, the gentle sound
Of her caressing voice in plaintive wave,
Past the green freshness where great willows lave,
And where the brightest of meadow flowers abound,
And smiled upon him that he find surcease,
Bringing to him a gentle sleep and peace.
Borne on the pinions of a dream, she gave

The music of her laughter, saying: "Sweet,
Mine Ilseus, the gods at last appeased
Take pity on your sufferings that eased
May be your agonizing. I repeat
That nowhere on the soil beneath the sun
Will you find remedy or truce, not one.
Such is the harsh law of your punishment.
Diana and her brother, Phoebus, will
Demand this for a stag you chanced to kill,
Forcing it on its course not long ago.
It came right to my brink a-dying slow,
An old stag that Diana loved and so
Hard pressed. Your javelin had sought its blood
That dripped, imprudent hunter, in my spring.
Its ebbing blood-tide was not for your good.
When killed at last, this victim did you bring
To me, the tree-tops trembling in their fright,
Its hapless, headless body, a dire sight.

"Long sobbed Diana, then she, for her spite
And for the blood slow spreading on the grass,
Brought you and for her vengeance to this pass.
Latona's children hate you without rest,
Pouring this ill upon your snowy breast.
Within this land, beneath their wrathful ban,
Your martyrdom is endless; but you can
Conserve your days at this abyss's brink.
Bring a black ram, and slit its throat and drink

Its blood at dawn and as a last resource,
Petition kindly Ops,[39] a last recourse,
To bring you aid. Then in the silent night
And in the shadows of the moon's pale light,
Pray to the unknown gods of this chill place
To waive their anger and to grant you grace,
And burning to them that you may appease,
Both thuja[40] and the twigs of cypress trees.

"Then, telling of your ills, a tender heart,
A nymph, sky-messenger, will come to hear
Your woes and she will guide you and impart
To you, adown a darkling road and drear,
The way to health. Now go! This is no lie.
Reality beneath a veil of dream
I'll show to you. Nymph of this spring am I.
Bathe in the verdant close's limpid stream.
Ilseus, in my waters must you lave,"
Quoth she, and then was lost in azure wave.
And for this prophecy, died his distresses.
With trembling hands a grateful heart he presses,
Crying: "O beautiful Callirrhoe,
E'er shall I follow when you call to me!"

Dawn with her roses tinged a saffron sky,
With Ilseus at a chasm's brink, hardby

---

[39] Ops was the Goddess of Pity and the wife of Saturn.
[40] There are five species of thuja, one in America, one in Africa, and the other three in China and Japan. All of them are evergreens.

Great bristling rocks where he would sacrifice,
Crying, and how his blood ran cold as ice:
"O Goddess Ops! Deign to accept my gift
Of blood." Night where its dusky shadows drift
He honored, and the gods of this abode,
With thuja and with cypress. Down the road
Of the abysmal void, a voice he hears
Reverberating. Chill is he for fears.
Loud as a thunder-clap, this awful sound
Causes the nymphs to swoon upon the ground.
Later they raise their supplicating hands
To let them fall again at Ops' commands,
Asking them all to end unending tasks
Of taming sulphurous wave that leaps and basks
As the quicksilver of the furroughed pool
Is mixed and hardened and then left to cool
To verigold, and in as pure a state
As gold may be without amalgamate.
And rays of air and flame produce with ease
The rich yield of the earth and of the seas,
Hiding beneath each bitter crest and stone
The secrets of alloy so swiftly grown
To the proportions of a mighty scale,
Flames rending an impenetrable veil.

Lipara, and by whom is made for us
Those vitalizing fires bituminous,
Rushing to Ilseus spake thus: "I know

Your every thought, intention, and your woe.
Cast fear away and to you let me say
That you may hope. I love Callirrhoe
Who will be crutch to these, your tottering days,
Bringing you to her many healing sprays
Hidden within the earth. At thick of night,
March on with rugged step, and toward the light."

And then she dragged him to a pitchy goal
Of yawning whirlpools. Terror struck his soul
Before such world-old chasms, every cave
Vomiting torrents with each murky wave.

Again she spake: "It's here that gods hold sway
In the earth's centre, very far from day.
Amongst the lower shades, Persephone
Reigns in her caverns underneath the sea.
Spilling their flames, they furrow as they fling
Them seaward, lightning ever vomiting.
Within this kingdom of my sisters, you
Shall see what human greed compels us to
Fashion. There gold and silver richly gleam.
Toward you, Callirrhoe will guide my stream.
Upon her fountain-breast too, I impress
The sulphurous vapors of our furnaces."

Ilseus, heeding her, took heart at this
And followed her unto a bleak abyss,

Wherein the crackling sulphur seethed, its glow
Consuming bronze where its white flames would go.
Then spake Lipara: "Metals here have birth,
Destined for greedy mortals of this earth.
And here a thousand goddesses like me
Engender all this wealth that you can see.
We consecrate the labor of our days,
Gathering our fires in a hundred ways,
Giving to brazier our live sparks indeed,
To mould a fine art that alloys be freed,
Amalgamated and imprisoned,
Reddening and glowing on their seething bed,
To plunge them finally in waters cool.

"Mount Aetna's roaring blasts are near this pool,
Where Vulcan's children have their smithy; where
Lava and smoke in marriage find the air.
Under the hammer, iron's servitude
Is tuned to mighty blows both harsh and rude.
The steep path to the forge lies to the left
(Follow my pointing hand) and at that cleft,
Pass to the right. Your body must you lave
Within the river's bright, metallic wave—
Heroic remedy. Now let us go
Down to that bank where gold veins lie below.
Tutty[a] illuminates its curving top,

---

[a] Tutty is an amphorous substance obtained as a sublimation product in the flues of smelting furnaces of zinc. It consists of crude zinc oxide.

And fuming sulphur, falling drop by drop,
Joins the wild whirlpool. Here's a sudden shift
Of aspect! That's quicksilver flowing swift.
Lave yourself thrice within its metal pool
That stretches there before you, none too cool."

Then splashing thrice with her white hand she gave
To Ilseus' body a quicksilvery wave.
And its result was swiftly purifying,
His ill consumed and for the metal's defying,
As over him this sacred fluid streamed,
Until his body of a sudden gleamed.
That which was soiled became so fresh and sweet.

"Now Ilseus, seek the skies on hurrying feet,
Bask in the sun again, breathe the pure air.
But your first thought must be, and your first care,
To give to Phoebe presents to appease
Her wrath and to the smithy's deities."

Thus spake Lipara. Drunk with gratitude,
Ilseus ran from whirlpool's metals crude,
And for this guiding nymph, toward radiant sun.
And how he thanked the gods, yes, every one!
The softest zephyrs played upon his breast,
As riffling breeze his golden hair caressed .

And unto twenty folk was soon revealed

Mercury's fame and what it had concealed
Of power, this liquid metal. When it unites
With hog's lard, soon it puts an one to rights,
And for a therapeutics all divine,
Especially when mixed with turpentine,[42]
And odorous resin of the lofty larch,
And horse's fat and bear's fat churned to starch,
Bdellium's juice and cedar's might intense,
Sulphur and myrrh and also frankincense.
And red lead is of benefit and we
Approve the mixture and should like to see
Iris and hellbore's black ingredient
With foetid lacebark and galbanum blent ,
And fluid juices of the mastic tree,
And oil of sulphur which is very fine,
Though it can lose in flames its power divine.

With hope departed, quickly must you spread
A thick coat on your body that it shed
Its loathesomeness, and do not fear its stain.
Thus the debasing evil can't remain.
Rub yourself well, but with a hand discreet,
Avoiding head and heart, right to the feet,
Missing no naked member, till a flax
Gives you a mane and coating soft as wax.
Beneath a weight of covers, sweat until[43]

---

[42] In Fracastoro's time, turpentine was used as a stimulant.
[43] In the early sixteenth century, sweating was held in high esteem in the cure of syphilis.

In dirty drops, has dripped away this ill.
Beneath these energetic agents' sway,
The virus finds a less corrosive way.
Though these be harsh, the evil is hard hit.
Now bathe your feet in water mixed with spit,
An unclean puddle which is bound to be
For your cure a most happy augury.

Within your mouth, ulcers you'll see anew,
But these will disappear and quickly too
Pure milk will deaden all their little dule.
Grenade in blossom, privet, as a rule,
Astringents harsh, salubrious will be,
Exterminating sores, and speedily.

For long an exile, Bacchus'll bring to you
A new strength for your body. This is true.
Falerno's wines and Corsica's will win
Fresh vigor for your once so-tainted skin.
Your ills will perish. Peace comes to your heart.
The azure skies their blessings now impart.
But one precaution, ere the work be done,
Rosemary and verbena must be one."
Also ally marjoram, celery, mint,
Giving a precious odor without stint.
Then bathe your body thrice within this pure
Solution, and complete will be your cure.

" All of these plants are rich in medicinal virtue and it is to be expected that
Fracastoro was greatly influenced by the pharmacopoeia of his day.

BOOK THREE

The new world calls to me that I may tell
Of forests where a magic treasure stands,⁴⁵
Past Hercules' Pillars and on distant strands,
Crossing, 'twixt poles, oceans that roar and swell.
Now would I sing of this so precious tree
Whose bark unknown to our forebears too will be
Borne from those distant bournes across the sea
To still the ravages of this new care.
Let its green foliage crown your sunny hair,
Divine Uranus! Deign to hear my vow,
In Epidaurus's cloak come you, and now.⁴⁶
Bring us this sacred tree that all adore,
Yea, show to us, and soon, this tree of trees
That gives rise to such wondrous prodigies,
This tree that Europe never saw before.⁴⁷

Let poets, moved by all these marvels too,
Then consecrate their vigils for the brave,
Reserving for their lutes that hero-crew
Whose ships audaciously cowed every wave,
Battling the seas and tempests without rest,
Yoking the oceans in a mighty quest.

---

⁴⁵ The *guaiacum officinale, lignum sanctum,* is a species of *lignum vitae,* once held as highly in esteem as mercury in the treatment for syphillis. For a short time, it looked as though this tree would dethrone its metallic rival. Infusions of its leaf and bark were given. This tree is a native of Brazil and of Santo Domingo, where it was first discovered.
⁴⁶ Epidaurus, a small town in Argolis, was the chief seat of the worship of Æsculapius, whose temple was situated about five miles distant from it.
⁴⁷ The *lignum sanctum* was first used in Spain as early as 1508, according to Delgado. Erasmus claims that its infusions cured him of the malady.

Newly discovered climates have been found,
And tropic skies and starry fires and bright
Illuminating all the veils of night.
Victory's wrested by a long sea-faring.
Now, vessels are to these new places bearing
Our names and laws, ploughing the stormy plain
Of ocean, furrowing its vast domain.
Our mariners, an all-victorious host,
Have cleaved the waters, steering down the coast.
The gods applaud this mighty work as great.
The slightest puff of wind will animate
My muse. These humble verses writ by me
Shall tell the old world of this kindly tree.

Where Phoebus leaves us, plunging in the brine;
Where Cancer stretches his long, torrid line,
An island,[48] conquered by the Spaniards, rises,
A goal for Spain and Spanish enterprises.

Vainly gold glitters there, a greater treasure
Is this tree that pours riches without measure,
The *lignum sanctum*, what a precious name!
And for its gifts it has a mighty fame.
No bitter frosts will turn its everliving
Greenness to grey. Its hoary head is giving

---

[48] This West Indian island, called Haiti, was discovered by Columbus on December 6, 1492. It was the first established seat of Europeans in America. The Spanish gave it the name of Hispaniola, or Little Spain, and there, in 1497, the town of Santo Domingo was founded.

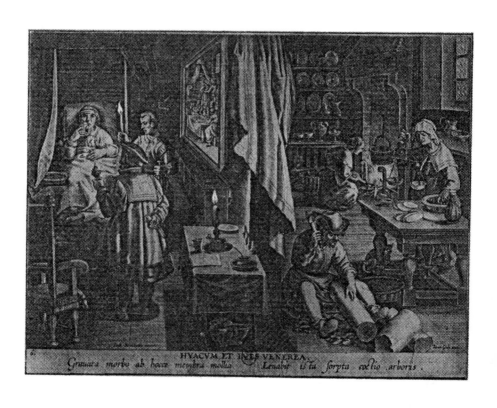

6.
HYACVM ET LVES VENEREA.
Grauata morbo ab hocce membra mollia   Lenabit ista forpta cœlio arboris.

Eternal foliage and colors bright.
And harsh and acid is its fruit. A sight
So beauteous is its fecund flowering.
Expose its trunk to flames and 'twill be showering
A sticky exhalation, resinous dew.
It has the weight and strength of iron too.
And like the laurel is its lustrous green.
Beneath its bark a so-pale coat is seen,
Yellow as boxwood. To describe its hue,
We must take ebony and walnut too,
Melting them till a reddish tint is seen,
Of iridescent and exquisite sheen.

And mourning rules this island where one sees
The ill I have described strike at the heart
Of all its folk, poor aborigines,
The *lignum sanctum* clothes its hills in part,
And clothes the plains to overcome this ill.
The grosser bark is stripped away until
It is reduced to dust right to its core.
Then fill a basin with pure water and
Soak the bark till it's soft and supple too.
Then put it on the flames, with skillful hand
To tend it till it foams. 'Twill never do
To let it boil beyond its cauldron's rim.
After it's boiled, the blessed foam then skim,
Spreading it on each abcess and each sore,
And covering them until they bleed no more.

And use this foam till all of it be spent
On limbs polluted and flesh purulent.
Half of this liquor will evaporate.
Divine's the draught that now is set to cool.
And might is given to it in boiling state.
The residue's mixed with honey as a rule.
And this drink must appear at every feast,
By order of the law and of the priest.
The energetic juices put away,
The sick must drink of them, yes, every day,
From nascent dawn that causes stars to pale,
Until the night has stretched her shimmering veil.
For long, the cup must not be put aside.
Night with her stars down slanting roads and wide,
Mixing her soft lights with the silvery ray
Of moonbeams, runs her course. Here comes the day!

But let the living seek a dark repose
Far from the chill of wind that fiercely blows,
Lest that it cool the sweat so humid steaming,
And for a regimen that's rigorous,
Taming a body once so vigorous,
Wherein its life is now so feebly gleaming.
It must have fast and hunger and the rest
That *lignum sanctum* pours into each breast,
A purer flame, a finer, healthier food,
Rival of high Olympus's so good,
Ambrosial, nectaral, and a food that saves,

Each time the lips have touched its blessed waves.
Two hours upon a captive couch must be
Endured by all, and sweating endlessly.
Then flies the malady and ulcer's pus
Is dried. The body grows more vigorous.
The *lignum sanctum* gives new life each day,
When Phoebe flings her down the Milky Way.

Lawless and aimless hazard ever plays
A part in this tree's many means and ways.
Gods made it known to savage folk. What's more,
A god once planted it upon this shore.
And where the Western Ocean touches night,
When Phoebus snuffs his torches flaming bright.

Led by a thirst for conquest, tempest-tossed,
Intrepid ships a heaving ocean crossed,
No signs within the skies, on seas appearing,
To aid these fearless sailors in their steering.
A troubled ocean, the Nereides,
Frightened by such intrepid ships as these,
Watched gilded poops streak paths as bright as fire,
Gloriously furrowing their vast empire.

On waves a-glitter through the night is seen
The moon's so-trembling and so-silvery sheen.
A hero countenanced by destiny,
First to approach these climes across the sea,

Gazes at heaven's vault and then he says:
"Phoebe, who rules the vast sea's humid ways,
Phoebe of ashen brow and paling head,
Twice have I seen you crescent, disc, then dead.
The land escapes me. Send me to some shore.
Our weary vessels can push on no more.
Offer some port to us, O heavenly queen,
Whose silent car lends night its silvery sheen!"

Latona's daughter, hearing this prayer, smiled
And left her throne of light and then beguiled
(Borrowing their beams) the Oceanides,
As they were gliding through the bitter seas.
Quoth she: "To-morrow, hero, shall you see
The land again. Your ships are dear to me.
But limit not your course to the first port.
Sail on, fate furthers you, and for my sport.
Ophyra must you find. It's my desire
That you stay there to found a great empire."

Then her hand pushed the vessels without rest,
Cleaving a path through ocean's heaving breast.
The wind became propitious. Ere the sun
Appeared above the fog, an isle was won,
Born of the mists, then looming larger and
Saluted with a frenzy by the band
Of mariners, who, rushing for the strand,
Reared altars there as a thank-offering too,

And tents and shelter for the tired crew.

When a fourth dawn has put the stars to flight,
The joyous sails are puffed by zephyrs light,
And jolly sailors, putting out to sea,
Beat the waves with their oars and merrily.
Cannibal Island's passed, then Anthylia's,
Gyana's verdant contours and Hagia's,
When suddenly above them towers rear
And rocks and forests. Many isles appear.
Beyond the panting seas is one so fair,
The tree-tops of its woods high in the air.
Hardby a fecund river too is found,
And glittering metals on its sands abound.
Cool springs there are and shady trees anigh
A charming spot beneath an azure sky.
The fleet casts anchor, joyous crews alight
And find upon these shores new, strange delight.
Some sacrifice to the Nereides,
And others would the island's gods appease.
Others set out to find what people live
Upon these wondrous shores the kind fates give.
And some go toward the stream in hopes 'twill hold
Their vessels. Others still would gather gold.

Not far from shore, upon a forest's breast
Azure and red-beaked birds are seeking rest
Upon their natal trees, a-fluttering there

And ever fearless and all unaware
Of danger. They are free and happy too.
But some imprudent sailors of the crew,
Seeing the creatures, tremble to let fly
The lightning mingled with the thunder's cry
From ardent arms from which destructions flare,
Impatient that they mingle with the air
Sulphur, saltpetre and the willow's coal,
Death concentrating in each brazen hole.

Upon a bird each sailor trains his eyes.
In twisted mesh a fuse well hidden lies.
As steel falls home, the kindling fires must leave
The guns, and whistling bullets rush to cleave
The air and victim birds lie on the ground.
Suddenly's heard the thunder to resound.
The skies aflame reverberate its roar.
And wrathful gods announce a vengeance for
Such ruthless carnage. Now have flown away
The birds. Safe in the thickets will they stay.
O miracle! Upon a branch one's swaying,
And to the trembling sailors it is saying:
"Ferocious Spaniards, your destructive hands
Profane birds that the sun protects in bands!
This forest has been soiled by your rash deed.
Apollo swears that it must be decreed
(After a thousand storms and dangers passed,
Reaching Ophyra's verdant shores at last)

That a new empire shall be ruled by you,
After great toil in many places too,
Constructing cities never seen before,
And curbing freedom neath a yoke of war,
That you shall wed with barren deeds and see
The ocean swallow all your fleet's debris,
Finding a thousand new graves every year,
For combats that will cost you many a fear.
And many a soldier will your land recruit,
To have him smashed to powder, and to boot,
Feel the forged lightnings of new Cyclopes,
Sowing among you discords that will freeze
Your very souls. Much blood your hands will spill,
The day arriving when your victims will
Regret this horrid crime, implore that it
May be forgotten, seek a benefit
Of this same forest." When the bird had made
This speech, it sought the thicket's deepest shade.
The sailors' blood ran cold and every one
Besought the birds' ghosts, the offended sun,
Ophyra's isle, the rustic gods, the stream,
Invisible guardians where the branches gleam,
To grant them peace. By gifts would they entice
A pardon. Eagerly they'd pay the price.

Then, toward the crew advanced an unknown race,
Unarmed, bare-breasted, walking with much grace.
As sign of peace, they waved green branches there.

Jet black and thick and waving was their hair.
To them our floating dwelling was so new,
Our shining weapons and our armor too,
Were captivating, dazzling to their eyes.
Thinking the Spaniards strange gods from the skies,
These noble-hearted aborigines
Raised fearful hands, adown upon their knees.
Also the heaven-sent chief would they entreat,
Bringing him honey, gold and fruit and wheat.
And in return, they got bright stuffs and many
Another present. Sparkling cups were quaffed,
With smoky wine therein, unknown to any
Of these kind savage folk. They drank and laughed
And warmed their hearts and made joy's wild ado.
'T would be the same, if any one of you
Was present at a banquet in the skies,
Fuddled with nectar, and with eager eyes
Gobbling the food reserved for gods alone,
Of such abundance that the tables groan.

Their fears abandoned and without constraint,
Soon were both peoples showing no restraint.
The chiefs embraced and lost was all defiance,
And publicly sworn to was a strict alliance.
Upon the dark breast of the savage chief,
There was an emerald cut in high relief,
And veils of gold. He bore a mighty spear
And standard that gave all the crew some fear.

This was a dragon's skin of hideous scale.
The white chief wore a suit of shining mail
And purple surcoat and a golden chain
That made the pallor of his skin more plain.
His helmet bore an eagle's feather white,
Toledo tempered was his sword and bright.
And in their games all vied so merrily.
All given over to hospitality.
Dwellings and vessels too were visited,
And, for the feasting, the hours so quickly sped.

Within the sacred wood, then everyone
Prepares an altar to the blazing sun,
Hardby the sea, within a gloomy dell,
And to it rush the ailing and unwell,
So sad of countenance, so sad of eye
And soiled of body, wet continuously
With foetid ichors that gods in their wrath
Visit upon this people's bitter path.
These people meet to make a sacrifice,
And priests wave *lignum-sanctum* leaves and spice
Dipped in the ocean's wave to cause a spray
Hoping the people's bane will pass away.
For bull's blood too, they hope that they'll be freed.
According to their very ancient creed,
They place this on a shepherd's forehead, one
A-nigh the altar. Chaunts rise to the sun,
The priests commencing these, the folk repeating.

Here, death of sheep and death of swine are meeting.
After the sacrifice the people feast
To Spain's astonishment, to say the least.
Seeing the wicked ravage of this ill,
Spaniards are struck with terror and until
The chief, recovering, cried: "This was predicted!"

Later the two folk met, still less restricted,
When each of them began to understand
The other, for the signs at their command.

Spain's chieftain and the savage island king
Soon found a means whereby the two might bring
An understanding, simple, to say the least.
The former asked: "This altar and this priest,
This shepherd and this blood, why are they there?"

The savage king replied: "Good Sir and fair,
My race has been condemned to suffering.
Year after year we make this offering,
An expiatory cult our fathers tried.
The gods and sun offended by the pride
Of our forefather's king, this evil came.
Therefore, this simple service has the aim
Of ending this so-noxious, fell disease
That fills our cities with its miseries.
Perchance the name of Atlas is known to you."

---

[49] Atlas, the son of Japetus and Clymene, warring with the other Titans against Zeus, was conquered and condemned to bear the heavens on his head and hands. He is supposed to be the father of the Pleiades, the Hyades, and the Hesperides. A more bitter fate was reserved for his brother, Prometheus, man-maker and flame-gatherer.

Our noblest king-ancestor is he too,
Our fathers springing from his royal blood.
Honoring the gods, he found them kind and good.
And we lived happily, until one day,
Our sons, corrupted by a wild display,
Overturned temples, scattering everything,
And tried the gods, vile insults squandering.
How they were punished for these mad excesses,
No word of mine, I fear, indeed expresses
The horror of the terror that avenges
The crime. Alas, the sun has his revenges!
You hardy mariners have heard the tale
Of fair Atlantis surely, without fail?
Queen of the earth, queen of the waves was she.
And Atlas gave this name to her and he
Brought her to luxury, until distress
Engulfed her in the waves whose bitterness
Spent all its fury on that feckless place.
With her there perished a gigantic race
Of cattle, men have sought to trace in vain,
A necessary offering that our bane
Vanish. We're victimized, our blood runs thick
With torture. Every one of us is sick.
Our flesh is torn. We are a living path
Of what the gods invented in their wrath
And visited upon us from the skies.
Our cult, an expiatory sacrifice,
Was made in hopes that we might end the mystery

Of this distemper. Let me give its history.

"An ancient king had we, Alcithous,
Who had a shepherd lad called Syphilus.
On our prolific meads, a thousand sheep,
A thousand kine this shepherd had to keep.
One day, old Sirius with his mighty flame,
During the summer solstice to us came,
Taking away the shade from all our trees,
The freshness from the meadow, coolth from breeze.
His beasts expiring, then did Syphilus
Turn to this horror of a brazen heaven,
Braving the sun's so torrid terror even,
Gazing upon its face and speaking thus:
'O Sun, how we endure, a slave to you!
You are a tyrant to us in this hour.
What matters it that bulls be killed, no few?
No father are you, nor supreme of power,
If fields be burned and sheep and kine and I.
Though jealous gods may never wish to see
Cattle submitted to my might, ah me,
My flocks are helpless for your brazen sky.
If the old tales be true, which is absurd,
You have one goat, one bull, and just one ram.
As guardian of this foolish little herd,
You have a mangy cur. The thing's a sham.
Why honor you? Alcithous is worth
Worship divine. He rules the sea and earth.

Stronger than gods and stronger than the sun,
He'll bring back verdant pastures, every one.
Life will he give to an expiring breeze,
He will revive the cattle and the trees.'

"Thus spake he. Braving gods, upon a hill
He reared an altar with a mighty will
To Prince Alcithous. The herdsmen bold
And all the ploughmen did as they were told,
Denying gods, deserting temples fair.
And to their king alone they worshipped there,
Reserving sacred bulls and frankincense
For him, and honoring him with joy immense.

"Upon his throne sat King Alcithous,
Whom a mad joy, alas, had blinded thus!
The outlawed gods no longer would he believe,
And he commanded that each state receive
Him as a god. Unto the thunder he sent
The gods, their cult — their domain his intent.

"But one who gazes, and with open eyes,
Embracing all the universe indeed,
Perceived the crime. Our island paradise
Received the evil of a subtle seed.
And foetid fogs and humid air became
The fardels of our impious, wicked shame.

"The sun went pallid for his righteous wrath
And germinated poisons on our path.
And he who wrought this outrage was the first
To feel his body ache, when sore accursed.
And for his ulcers and their torturing,
No longer would a tossing, hard couch bring
Him sleep. With joints apart and flesh erased,
Thus was the shepherd flailed and thus debased.
And after him this malady we call
SYPHILIS,[50] tearing at our city's wall
To bring with it such ruin and such a wrack,
That e'en the king escaped not its attack.

"The folk in fear, within the wood, Carthesis
Ran to consult the dryad, Ameresis.
Behind a clump of trees was her retreat.
Infallible, interpretive and sweet
Was she. They asked why gods condemned them and
Whom should they seek to cure them. She replied:
'All of the gods are wrathful. Understand,
Perverted race, you perish for your pride.
You braved the sun. The sun has punished you.
Incense is not for man. Immortals too
Find this a horror. You were prideful, mad.
Erect once more your altars and be glad
That sacrificial flesh shall smoke again.
Immortal justice is not stayed by men.

[50] The word may be derived from the Greek: sus-philos which means hog-love.

Your punishment must be eternal bane.
Apollo swears this by the sacred Styx.
He'll ease this ravage if you lunatics
Will worship gods again. To banish pain,
The sky reserves a mighty remedy
For you born of these shores. A black cow's blood
To Tellus[51] must be poured upon the grass.
And a white heifer might change Juno's mood,
Ere aught be granted that this ill may pass.
Some fecund seeds in Tellus's vast breast
Can grow a wide and leafy tree to scorn
This poison's energy. Peace! Be at rest!
Tellus will see that this tree shall be born.'

"Silent grew Ameresis and the sun
Sought the soft couch of west. The trees, the caves
Trembled at her soft voice when day was done.
The people reared their altars by the waves.
Juno and Tellus were given sacrifices.
O miracle! Anon, a great tree rises,
And, by the gods, it was not seen before,
By any people living on this shore.
The fertile land was shaded by this tree,
Covering our fields and hillsides, every lea.
And temples were reopened to the sun.
For expiation, all the gods chose one

---

[51] *Tellus mater* is the ancient Latin deity of earth. She was the Goddess of marriage and of fertility and she was invoked in solemn oaths as the grave of all things. Several festivals were celebrated in her honor.

Poor victim for a folk so impious;
Their common choice, the shepherd, Syphilus.
He bent his head beneath a sacred band,
Resigned and calm. And then, at a command,
The steel is raised to make his blood to flow.
But Juno turns the sword aside and so
The execution's stayed and by her grace.
Apollo's bull shall take the shepherd's place.

"Our fathers founded this so solemn rite,
Hoping to expiate a crime thereby.
And good are all the gods who dwell on high,
And every year they gather for this sight,
And every year a shepherd symbolizes
The victim; ancient are these sacrifices.
Each generation celebrates this feast.
It never ceases and our punishment
Continues 'til some clemency is sent
To us by all the gods. This crowd and priest
Assemble that the people purify
Them by infusions of this sacred tree,
In hopes to quench the fires for which they die,
When blazes in them this fierce malady."

After this dissertation, every one,
Each friendly for the moment, went away.
The Spaniards sought their vessels that same day,
Fearing the scourge. And quickly did they run

To seek the summer skies of their dear land,
Save those who stayed and at their chief's command.
Thus Europe is delivered to the plague
Of fair Ophyra, distant land and vague.
And questions science for this evil vile,
But science answers not, nor will she smile.

Sinister fleet, you plough a noisy sea,
Minister of an evil destiny
Are you, implacable, developing
A plague that unto Spain will swiftly bring
Death or black misery. The sailors hit
By this dread malady will die of it,
Or, what is worse, infect full many a city.
Implore the ancient forest to have pity.
Where blood is sacrificed beneath the trees,
Stay rage, O sun! Let hamadryades
Sacrifice too, and in a manner august.
Also the *lignum-sanctum* stem you must
Cull, lest disaster fall on every one,
For a bird-murder and an outraged sun.

Spaniards, take your Ophyra's customs home
And quaff the cup containing sparkling foam
And drink the branches' juices with a will,
That by this means you may forget your ill.

Mariners, carry to your fatherland

This wood that stays the furthering of this evil,
Consigning it to Hell and to the Devil.
Go with this precious tree, a little band,
Delivering from this horror Europe's skies.
Pushed by a happy wind, your vessel flies
Over the seas whose rage is calmed by one
Phoebus-Apollo, Lord-God of the Sun.

Destiny chooses you, O Spain sublime,
To bring this treasure of a distant clime!
All Italy and Germany and France
And Scythia—all of these look askance
Upon this fester. All of them implore
The *lignum-sanctum* of that distant shore.
And throughout Europe at this plague 'twill hit,
Sowing the wonder of its benefit.

Hail, you whose leaves are rising toward the skies!
Hail, you whose sap contains sweet wizardies!
Tree that the Sun-God planted with his hand
You are the new-world glory that has banned
A misery that humans may have hope!
All hail! All hail! Our country's miseries
Will vanish when are sown these sacred trees.
Let Latium grow this blessed foliage
And go in peace. No Muse inspires me
To send you to the frozen arctic sea,
To Turkestan and Ammon's realm. Your fame

I'll foster ever, singing your sweet name.
To the Adige's waves, my feeble voice
Repeats your miracle that all rejoice.

Now lend your fame to this old universe,
Mingle your name, O Bembo, with my verse,
That lignum-sanctum's marvels may be shown
And that my vigil's findings may be known!

FINIS

APPENDIX

IACTA EST ALEA

HVLDERICVS AB HVTTEN, EQVES ET
POETA NOBILISSIMVS
Qvi res Marte gerit digna, et qui bene gestas
Arte canit, Lauri munerä uterqȝ capit.
HVTTENI utrumȝ meres, Eqpitum lux, gloria Vatum,
Nam duplicas gen ȝ nobilitate genus.

E.Kiefer exc.   Dan. Meisn.C.B.

THE ORIGIN OF THE FRENCH DISEASE*

In our times, Providence wills that one sees maladies that were unknown to our forefathers, or so, many men believe. About 1493 A.D., there burst upon us this pestilential evil, nor was it in France, but in the kingdom of Naples that it exploded. If it has received the name, "The French Disease," it is because it appeared for the first time in the French Expeditionary Force that fought in Italy under the command of King Charles. Regarding this accusation as an injury, France has repudiated it and has called the malady the Neapolitan Evil. Nevertheless, according to prevailing usage, I shall call the malady the French Disease in this tract, through no hatred of a celebrated nation which is perhaps today the most civilized and the most hospitable that exists, but because I fear that I shall not be understood by my readers, should I give a different name to this malady that a superstition concerning its origin has given rise to.

Certain folks have called it *mevium*, the name of a saint with whom I am not familiar. Other people like to believe that this is Job's malady. Still others would call it after Evagrius who is supposed to have been affected by this ill. This monk of the desert, exposed to all of the rigors of the seasons, lived on herbs and raw roots, his body being covered by a herpetic eruption. Many pilgrims have visited his chapel, carrying valuable offerings there. Such were the reigning theories in these moments of terror. Some folk maintained even that the malign ulcers were no more than a recrudescence of the malady of Saint Roch.

---

* Translated into French in *Æsculape*, (Vol. 7, No. 4, April, 1926) from Uldrich von Hutten's *De guaia medicina et morbo gallico*, Jo Schoeffer, Mainz, 1519.

If this be a true religious sentiment that has propagated these beliefs, I am far from blaming it; but if this be a motive of self interest, a hope to draw a benefit, I flay it and those cheats by whom the human race has been victimized in the midst of a terrific public calamity.

According to the theologians, God has seminated this malady in anger and in order to punish creatures whose vices have outraged His Majesty. The priests have preached these doctrines from the pulpit, as though they had been revealed to them by the Almighty Who had called them into His council-halls. Quoth they: "Never had men been so perverse."

The century of Augustus and of Tiberius, when Jesus was crucified, was it really an age of gold? Is it not possible that spontaneously the forces of the nature of new maladies could develop under particular circumstances? Every day, do we not see essential changes in facts that cause them to operate differently than has been their custom? Has it not been proven for at least two years, that we are no better off for the discovery of guaiacum, which is supposed to be a sovereign remedy for the malady?

The conduct of the physicians has been similar to that of the priests, and instead of searching for remedies that might cure, they have pretended to seek causes, and actually have fled from the presence of the people who have been stricken with this ill, and have refrained from touching them. In general, the symptoms of the malady were so terrible, so contagious, but now the conditions are not the same as they were at first.

Pustules and ulcerations show themselves on all parts of the body, so hard and wrinkled that they may be compared to glands of oak, both because of their greatness and their shape. From them oozes an ichorous pus that is so foetid that one believes that the very odor is capable of provoking the contagion. These pustules have a greenish tint bordering on black. The victims suffer as much from the hideous state in which they find them as from the actual pains by which they are overwhelmed. They become the prey of a torture as cruel as that of being cast into the fire.

The ill once sowed, spread over Germany with a greater violence and rapidity than anywhere, the people's habits of drunkenness and debauchery favoring its propagation to the highest degree.

Those savants who consulted the stars predicted that the scourge would last only seven years; but they have made a profound mistake. Had they announced that after this period, the malady would disappear, or at least its symptoms would disappear in an individual who had contracted it, they would have been correct. Furthermore, they would not have been wrong had they stated that the virulence and contagion would lose their initial intensity. For it must be acknowledged that the malady retains all of its energy for seven years only. Then it modifies to become what it is at present, less malign in its sway, less horrible in appearance, although the indurated flesh is ploughed and invaded. The virus persists, still dangerous, but its effects are less rapid, its infiltrations less ample and it engenders numerous maladies and much degeneration of the tissues. But at this moment, no one contracts the malady, unless exposed to it directly. The disease in general is caught by sexual contact. Children and old people are more rarely infected. Predisposed to it are the luxury-lover and the libertine. If the vicious contract it, they will languish and die slowly, the victims of their excesses. Italians, Spanish, and folk more sober than ourselves, more reserved, have less to suffer. Drunkenness and libertinage of any kind engender and increase this evil in us.

For a long time the matter of occult causation has been discussed by physicians and is far from being solved. There is an extreme divergence of sentiment, and that they are in accord on one point alone is easy to understand. Some affirm, in these unfortunate times, that the air suddenly charges itself with miasmas and that an impure wind has corrupted the waters of lakes, fountains, rivers and even seas, and that the earth has become infected and that pestilential vapors have not spared even the animals and that morbid influences have touched many of them.

The astrologers who pretend to explain everything by the movement of the stars, trace the epidemic to the conjunction of Mars and Saturn that had taken place a short time before its outburst. They have rejected as cause, the two eclipses of the sun observed by certain people who attributed its cause to this. According to them, these eclipses can only presage mucus, biliousness and long, chronic, stubborn maladies, such as elephantiasis, leprosy, impetigo, malignant herpes, and disorders that deform the body, such as gout, rheumatism, paralysis, pains in the limbs, in short, all lesions of this nature.

Many physicians advance the theory that the malady was engendered by an internal, tainted principle, by corrupted humors, melancholic dessicatedness, by yellow bile or by phlegm that had been burned or salted. And it is possible that all of these profound troubles can take place at the same time, pernicious elements, ranged to dispose themselves on the exterior envelope of the body, the skin that has been ulcerated and destroyed; members being penetrated by liquids decomposed and corrupted, suffering bursting as soon as the tumors show themselves and nodosities and tubercules uncover the skin, even that of the head, the constitution compromised and mined in its entirety.

Other physicians, without entering into any thorough explanation, are contented to tell us that the scourge is an infection caused by the corruption of the blood. Laying aside vague discussions on the incomprehensible essence of the malady, they would tell us that it is the consequence of the depravity of the blood which has become purulent in some way, and which is manifested by swellings, ulcerations and concretions. Still others tell us that the source of this disorder comes from some trouble with the functioning of the liver, or from an alteration in this organ itself.

The only point in which our physicians can be in accord is that the malady dates from our epoch. For the first two years after its appearance, the German physicians did not wish to commit themselves and, therefore, kept silent. I was still a young man when they undertook to cure me. The deplorable results obtained prove the powerlessness of the means that they employed. I remember that it was forbidden me to eat peas because I was told that these grains could enclose little winged insects that cause the infection. Also pork was forbidden and the flesh of other animals which caused chemical changes that were considered dangerous.

NOTES ON ILLUSTRATIONS

TITLE PAGE

Portrait of Girolamo Fracastoro from Homocentrica, Venice, 1538. Printer, Francesco Marcolini. Courtesy of The National Library, Paris.

PAGE xii

Engraved by Nicholas de Larmessin, the elder, born at Paris, 1640. Courtesy of The National Library, Paris.

PAGE xxvi

Woodcut by Albrecht Durer, 1490, supposed to be the first illustration depicting syphilis. Courtesy of AESCU-LAPE, Paris.

PAGE 20

Mercurial treatment for syphilis, Amsterdam, 1696. Courtesy of AESCULAPE, Paris.

PAGE 28

Columbus's flagship, woodcut made at Basle, 1494. Courtesy of AESCULAPE, Paris.

PAGE 34

Engraved by Jacques Lagniet, Paris, 1659. Courtesy of AESCULAPE, Paris.

PAGE 44

Courtesy of the National Library, Paris.

PAGE 58

Administering the lignum sanctum. Illustration by Stradanus engraved by Gallus. Courtesy of AESCULAPE, Paris.

Page 76

Woodcut by Conrad Reitter, 1508. The Virgin invoked to prevent syphilis. Courtesy of AESCULAPE, Paris.

Page 78

Syphilis and her attendants. Courtesy of AESCULAPE, Paris.

Page 80

Uldrich von Hutten, Knight, courtesy of The National Library, Paris.

One Thousand Copies Printed by Ward Ritchie, 1934

Printed in the United States
89632LV00006B/145/A